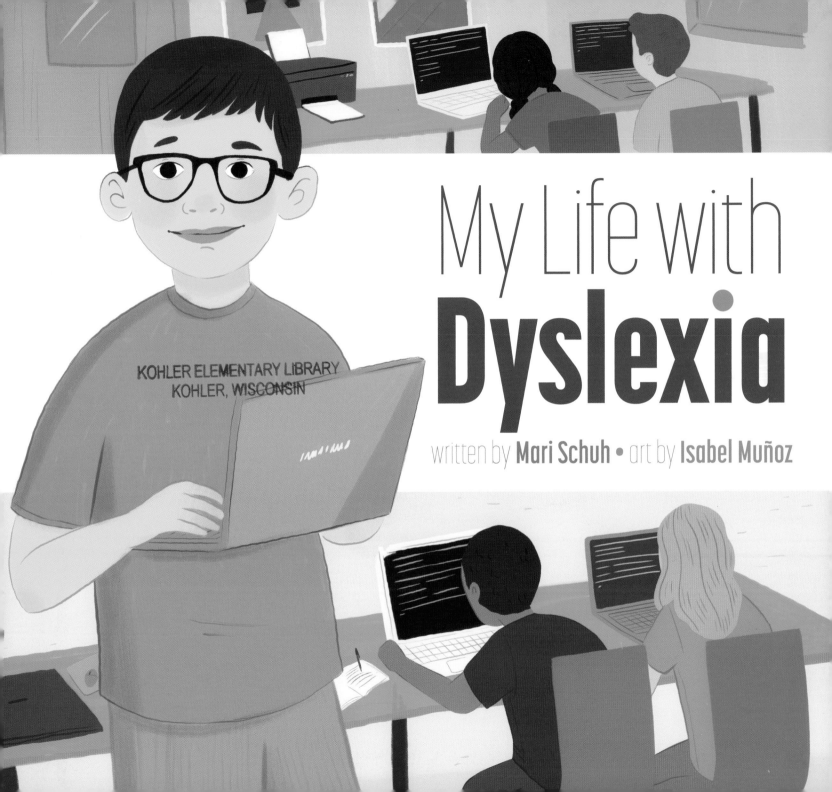

My Life with
Dyslexia

written by **Mari Schuh** • art by **Isabel Muñoz**

AMICUS ILLUSTRATED and AMICUS INK
are published by Amicus
P.O. Box 1329, Mankato, MN 56002
www.amicuspublishing.us

Editor: Gillia Olson
Designer: Kathleen Petelinsek

Library of Congress Cataloging-in-Publication Data
Names: Schuh, Mari C., 1975- author. | Muñoz, Isabel, illustrator.
Title: My life with dyslexia / by Mari Schuh ; illustrated by Isabel Muñoz.
Description: Mankato, Minnesota : Amicus, [2021] | Series: My life with... | Includes bibliographical references. | Audience: Ages 6-9 |
Audience: Grades 2-3 | Summary: "Meet Scott! He likes coding and playing basketball. He also has dyslexia. Scott is real and so are his
experiences. Learn about his life in this illustrated narrative nonfiction picture book for elementary students"—Provided by publisher.
Identifiers: LCCN 2019048141 (print) | LCCN 2019048142 (ebook) | ISBN 9781681519944
(library binding) | ISBN 9781681526416 (paperback) | ISBN 9781645490791 (pdf)
Subjects: LCSH: Dyslexia—Juvenile literature. | Dyslexic children—United States—Biography—Juvenile literature.
Classification: LCC RJ496.A5 S36 2021 (print) | LCC RJ496.A5 (ebook) | DDC 618.92/8553—dc23
LC record available at https://lccn.loc.gov/2019048141
LC ebook record available at https://lccn.loc.gov/2019048142

Printed in the United States of America

HC 10 9 8 7 6 5 4 3 2 1
PB 10 9 8 7 6 5 4 3 2 1

For Scott and his family-MS

About the Author
Mari Schuh's love of reading began with cereal boxes at
the kitchen table. Today, she is the author of hundreds of
nonfiction books for beginning readers. With each book, Mari
hopes she's helping kids learn a little bit more about the world
around them. Find out more about her at marischuh.com.

About the Illustrator
To paint for a living was Isabel Muñoz' dream, and now she's
proud to be the illustrator of several children books. Isabel
works from a studio based in a tiny, cloudy, green and lovely
town in the north of Spain. You can follow her at isabelmg.com.

Hey there! I'm Scott. I'm a smart, fun kid like you. I play basketball and I like computers. We might have some differences, too. I have dyslexia. Let me to tell you a little bit about my life.

People with dyslexia have trouble with language. It can be hard to read, write, and spell. Kids with dyslexia are born with it. People are more likely to have it if someone in their family has it, too. My mom and brother both have dyslexia.

People with dyslexia want to read and learn. But their brains have a tough time connecting letters to the sounds they make. Their brains might mix up letters in a word. It might add or leave out letters. People with dyslexia might not say words in the right way. They could have a hard time learning words that rhyme.

Dyslexia affects me in other ways, too. I have trouble finding the right word to say. So I say *stuff* and *things* a lot. I have a tough time knowing left from right. And I often forget the name of my street.

8

My writing is messy, so I use an erasable pen to erase my mistakes. It's also hard for me to tell time. So I use a digital clock.

At school, my teacher breaks up my work into smaller parts. She gives me more time to do my work. I take tests in a quiet, empty classroom so I can focus.

At home, I use a ruler that highlights words as I read. I also listen to audiobooks. Speech to text on a computer is helpful, too. It types the words I say onto the screen.

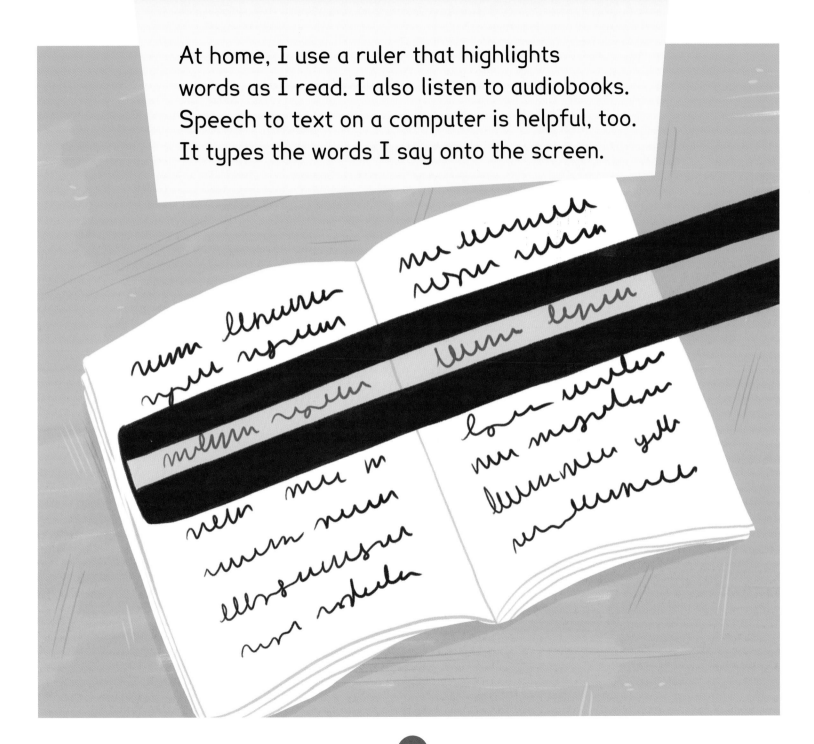

Reading is hard work. I have to take breaks. Mom jokes with me to help me relax. I hang out with my cat. My friend Emma also helps me. She is quiet and calm, which makes me feel better.

Words seem to be everywhere! So dyslexia affects me outside of school, too. It's tough to read signs at football games or other events.

Reading menus causes me trouble. I read the words wrong and ask for the wrong food. The server gets confused. I get upset. I need more time to get the words right. Mom helps me.

People with dyslexia can be sensitive to how other people feel. Struggling to read can make me sad. I want to help people who are struggling. When my school got rid of old books, I helped out. I gave the books to kids who don't have many.

I'm also saving money to buy food for people who need it.

People with dyslexia have a unique way of thinking. I love to code. I've learned how to give computers the instructions to do all kinds of things. Coding has reading and typing. But a big part of coding is solving problems. My brain is good at that. Last summer, I went to coding camp. I had tons of fun!

My family often plays games together. At first, it was hard to read and learn the rules. I worked hard and kept trying. Now I'm really good at lots of games. I have fun!

Meet Scott

Hi! I'm Scott. I live in Connecticut with my mom, dad, brother, and sister. We have a cat named Marshall. I like to play in the woods, ride my scooter, and go to summer camp. Swimming and playing video games are also fun. Because I love everything about computers, I want to work with computers when I grow up. I plan to be a software engineer.

Respecting People with Dyslexia

If a kid with dyslexia is having trouble reading, be patient. They are trying their best. They might need extra time.

Be friendly to people with dyslexia. Don't bully them or make fun of them. Treat them how you would like to be treated.

Reading in a front of a classroom can be tough for people with dyslexia. Don't laugh or make fun. Be kind and listen.

Everyone has things they are good at and things they like to do. The same is true for people with dyslexia.

Dyslexia affects more than a person's reading. People with dyslexia might have a hard time telling time. They also might not be able to tell left from right. Be kind and help if they ask.

Helpful Terms

audiobook A recording of a person reading a book aloud.

coding Programming a computer to follow a set of instructions.

focus To keep your attention on something or someone.

language The words that people use to talk and write to one another.

rhyme Words that end with the same sound.

sensitive Easily hurt or affected by small changes or differences.

struggle To have a hard time doing something.

unique Unlike others.

Read More

Miller, Connie Colwell. **You Can Respect Differences: Assume or Find Out?** Making Good Choices. Mankato, Minn.: Amicus, 2020.

Pettiford, Rebecca. **Different Interests**. Celebrating Differences. Minneapolis: Bullfrog Books, 2018.

Squire, Ann. **Dyslexia**. A True Book. New York: Children's Press, an imprint of Scholastic Inc., 2017.

Websites

BBC: COPING WITH DYSLEXIA: SOPHIE'S STORY

https://www.bbc.co.uk/teach/class-clips-video/pshe-ks2-coping-with-dyslexia-sophies-story/zdvr8xs

Nine-year-old Sophie talks about what it's like to have dyslexia.

KIDSHEALTH: DYSLEXIA

https://kidshealth.org/en/kids/dyslexia.html

Learn more about reading and dyslexia.

WONDEROPOLIS: WHAT IS DYSLEXIA?

https://www.wonderopolis.org/wonder/what-is-dyslexia

Find helpful information about dyslexia.

Every effort has been made to ensure that these websites are appropriate for children. However, because of the nature of the Internet, it is impossible to guarantee that these sites will remain active indefinitely or that their contents will not be altered.